Tobias Catches Trout

by Ole Hertz

Translated from the Danish by Tobi Tobias

Carolrhoda Books, Inc.   Minneapolis

This edition first published by Carolrhoda Books, Inc., 1984
Original edition first published by The Danish National Museum, Copenhagen, 1981
under the title TOBIAS FISKER ØRRED
Copyright © 1981 by Ole Hertz
English translation copyright © 1984 by Tobi Tobias
All rights reserved.
Published in agreement with International Children's Book Service, Copenhagen, Denmark
Manufactured in the United States of America

LIBRARY OF CONGRESS CATALOGING IN PUBLICATION DATA

Hertz, Ole.
   Tobias catches trout.

   Translation of: Tobias fisker ørred.
   Summary: Tobias, a young Greenlander, goes on a trout
fishing expedition with his family in their motor boat.
   [1. Greenland—Fiction. 2. Fishing—Fiction]
I. Tobias, Tobi. II. Title.
PZ7.H432463T   1984   [E]   83-27224
ISBN 0-87614-263-3 (lib. bdg.)

1 2 3 4 5 6 7 8 9 10 93 92 91 90 89 88 87 86 85 84

Tobias is twelve years old.
He lives in Greenland with his mother and father,
his big sister, and his little brother.

Here is the house Tobias lives in.
His father and mother built it themselves
from wooden boards.

One day Tobias and his father and mother,
his sister, and his brother get their motorboat ready.
They are going to sail up the fjord to a stream
where they will fish for trout.

There are many things they must remember to take along:
the primus stove to cook their food on,
crackers, flour, rice, sugar, coffee, matches, kerosene,
gasoline, nets, a tent, blankets, and comforters.
It is best not to forget anything, for then
they would have to sail all the way back again to get it.

They set out.
The sea is smooth and shining.
Although it is summer,
it's cold sitting still in the boat.
They must sail for several hours
before they get to the fishing place.

At last, after all of them are stiff with cold,
they get there.
Tobias helps put up the tent,
and in a little while they can all warm themselves
with the soup his mother has made.

The next day Tobias and his father set out the trout nets.
Tobias's big sister and little brother and mother
build an oven out of clay and sod and old cloth bags.
They must also collect heather for fuel.
The trout will be smoked in the oven so they will keep better.

Tobias and his father catch a lot of trout.

The trout are cleaned and hung on sticks.
Then they are smoked for a night and a day.
Tobias also helps collect heather for the oven.

One night a wind comes up.
It shakes and jerks the tent.
Finally they have to take the poles down
so the tent won't blow away.

The next morning the wind has died down.
Tobias is the first to crawl out.
Quickly they raise the tent again.

The next day they pack up the tent
and carry all the smoked fish onto the boat.
Then they start for home.

First they sail to the town
and sell most of the trout.
People from the town
come down to the harbor to buy their fish.

Afterward, Tobias and his family hurry to sail home.
The town is very noisy, and besides,
some of the people there laughed at them
because they did not talk like the townspeople.

At last they are home in their settlement again.

Everyone who comes to welcome them gets a fish.

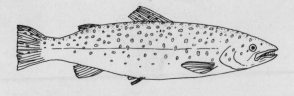

People fish with trout nets in streams and lakes and at those places along the coast where streams flow into fjords or the sea. Today most of the nets are made of nylon and are bought from stores in fishing villages. They are equipped with floats which hold them up just below the surface of the water, because that is where the trout live. One end of the net is tied securely on land; the other end is anchored with a stone. The fisherman sails out on the water, dropping the net little by little, then drops the stone to the bottom of the water. More fish are caught if the net is emptied several times a day so that the trout that swim by aren't frightened off by the ones already caught in the net.

A full-grown Greenlandic trout is about 50 centimeters (20 inches) long and weighs about 2 kilograms (4⅖ pounds). The trout live in streams until they are about four years old. Then they begin to migrate. They live in the sea in the summer, but each autumn they return to the streams in which they grew up.

There are also trout that live their whole lives in lakes. In fresh water the trout live on insects, snails, and sticklebacks. In the sea they live on crayfish, smaller fish, and newly hatched fish.

Trout are found all along Greenland's coast. They are caught mostly for home consumption, but in some places also for export.